# The MAGNA CARTA

By Janey Levy

**Gareth Stevens**
Publishing

Please visit our website, www.garethstevens.com. For a free color catalog of all our high-quality books, call toll free 1-800-542-2595 or fax 1-877-542-2596.

**Library of Congress Cataloging-in-Publication Data**

Levy, Janey.
The Magna Carta / by Janey Levy.
  p. cm. — (Documents that shaped America)
Includes index.
ISBN 978-1-4339-9002-1 (pbk.)
ISBN 978-1-4339-9003-8 (6-pack)
ISBN 978-1-4339-9001-4 (library binding)
1. Magna Carta—Juvenile literature. 2. Constitutional history—Great Britain—Juvenile literature. I. Levy, Janey. II. Title.
JN147.L48 2014
942.033—d23

First Edition

Published in 2014 by
**Gareth Stevens Publishing**
111 East 14th Street, Suite 349
New York, NY 10003

Copyright © 2014 Gareth Stevens Publishing

Designer: Sarah Liddell
Editor: Therese Shea

Photo credits: Cover, pp. 1, 11 Duncan Walker/E+/Getty Images; pp. 5, 28 Hulton Archive/Stringer/Hulton Archive/Getty Images; p. 6 DEA PICTURE LIBRARY/De Agnosti Picture Library/Getty Images; p. 7 Spanish School/The Bridgeman Art Library/ Getty Images; p. 8 Nick Hewetson/Getty Images; pp. 9, 14, 26 Popperfoto/Contributor/ Popperfoto/Getty Images; pp. 12, 15 English School/The Bridgeman Art Library/ Getty Images; p. 13 Universal Images Group/Contributor/Universal Images Group/ Getty Images; p. 16 Marcus Gheeraerts/The Bridgeman Art Library/Getty Images; p. 17 Peter Tillemans/The Bridgeman Art Library/Getty Images; p. 18 photo courtesy of Wikimedia Commons, Petition of Right.jpg; p. 19 DEA/A. DE GREGORIO/Contributor/ De Agnosti Picture Library/Getty Images; p. 21 Hulton Archive/Stringer/Archive Photos/ Getty Images; p. 22 photo courtesy of Wikimedia Commons, Massachusetts state seal 1775 1780 MassachusettsArchives.png; p. 23 John Parrot/Stocktrek Images/ Getty Images; p. 24 Steve McAlister/Photographer's Choice/Getty Images; p. 25 photo courtesy of Wikimedia Commons, Washington Constitutional Convention 1787.jpg; p. 27 Photri Images/SuperStock/Getty Images.

Printed in the United States of America

CPSIA compliance information: Batch #CS13GS: For further information contact Gareth Stevens, New York, New York at 1-800-542-2595.

# CONTENTS

Words in the glossary appear in **bold** type the first time they are used in the text.

# AN IDEA IS BORN

Have you heard the saying "The pen is mightier than the sword"? It means words and ideas are so powerful they can change the world—and are even more effective than weapons and force. One of the best examples of this saying is a **document** called the Magna Carta.

Written in England in 1215, the Magna Carta is now considered one of the most important and influential writings in history. Its name is Latin for "great **charter**," and it grew out of conflict between British barons and King John. The barons had grown unhappy with the king's **abuses** of power and forced him to sign this promise of their rights. As unlikely as it might seem, this 800-year-old document helped shape the United States years later.

## It's a Fact!

Runnymede was the site of the historic meeting of King John and the British barons.

4

# RUNNYMEDE

The barons and King John met at a place called Runnymede on June 15, 1215. Most people think this is where John signed the Magna Carta, but that's not accurate. What John signed at Runnymede was a list of the barons' complaints and demands called the Articles of the Barons. Four days later, after changes were made, both sides approved the final document. That's what became known as the Magna Carta.

# MEDIEVAL ENGLISH SOCIETY

To understand the Magna Carta, it helps to know about **medieval** England. Like other European countries, England was a feudal society. "Feudalism" was the medieval military and political system.

In feudalism, the king owned all the land. Below the king were the barons. The king granted each baron a plot of land to use called a fief. But the king still owned the land. In return for the fief, the baron pledged his loyalty and service to the king. He also provided either knights or money for the king's wars. At the bottom of society were peasants, who lived on the baron's fief and farmed it for him. The barons and peasants were all vassals, or subjects, of the king.

## It's a Fact!

Occasionally quarrels were settled in a trial by combat, with the arguing barons actually fighting each other. The winner of the fight was declared the winner of the quarrel.

Some powerful barons had their own small armies. This meant it wasn't easy for the king to control them.

## THE FEUDAL JUSTICE SYSTEM

Quarrels among the barons were settled at the king's court, which was composed of all the barons and overseen by the king. As a group, the barons made decisions to resolve the quarrels. Barons involved in quarrels were required to obey a summons, or an order to appear in court. If a baron refused to appear or disobeyed the court's decision concerning the quarrel, the king could take back

# A TYRANT KING

John became king in 1199 and was soon at war with France. By 1206, John had lost England's territories in France. He waged war for 10 years, trying unsuccessfully to regain those lands.

Taxes rose steeply to finance the war, angering the barons. Barons who didn't provide knights had to pay three times the normal fee. Those who didn't pay were fined. John also heavily taxed the barons' land and household possessions.

John angered the barons in other ways, too. He didn't trust his nobles. He kept close watch over their land and income. John launched wars against barons he thought were plotting against him. By 1215, the barons had had enough. They presented their demands to John in the Articles of the Barons.

Robin Hood

## A TROUBLED YOUTH

Even before John became king, his actions had made enemies and raised questions about his fitness to rule. His father, Henry II, sent young John to rule Ireland. John behaved so irresponsibly that he was forced to return to England after only 6 months. After the death of Henry II, John's older brother Richard the Lionhearted became king. While Richard was away at war, John tried unsuccessfully to steal the throne from him.

King John spent large sums of money to support a luxurious lifestyle, and this further angered the barons.

# BARONS' RIGHTS and the KING'S POWER

The Magna Carta wasn't the first charter to recognize the rights of the barons. Earlier kings had issued similar charters. But the earlier charters had been freely granted, while the barons forced the Great Charter on King John. This difference was vital. Unlike the earlier charters, the Magna Carta was a challenge to the king's authority.

The Magna Carta consists of a preamble, or introduction, and 63 clauses, or articles, dealing with several topics. The subjects include feudal laws of special concern to the barons, issues concerning towns and merchants, reform of the law and of justice, and behavior of royal officials. The final clauses give the barons the right to take action against the king if he doesn't obey the charter. In other words, even the king wasn't above the law.

## It's a Fact!

Most clauses in the Magna Carta deal with specific complaints rather than general principles of law. For example, clause 33 promises to improve river navigation by removing pens, or weirs, placed in the waterways to catch fish.

John's own father, Henry II, had issued a charter making promises to the barons.

## ROYAL OFFICIALS MUST OBEY THE LAW

(30) No sheriff, royal official, or other person shall take horses or carts for transport from any free man, without his consent.

(31) Neither we [the king] nor any royal official will take wood for our castle, or for any other purpose, without the consent of the owner.

(38) In future no official shall place a man on trial upon his [the official's] own unsupported statement, without producing **credible** witnesses to the truth of it.

Clause 39 promises due process, which is the practice of applying laws fairly, and the right to judgment by one's peers. Clause 40 promises the right of prompt justice. Clauses 39 and 40 are regarded today as especially important promises of rights and liberty:

(39) No free man shall be seized or imprisoned, or stripped of his rights or possessions, or outlawed or exiled, or **deprived** of his standing in any other way, nor will we [the king] proceed with force against him, or send others to do so, except by the lawful judgment of his equals or by the law of the land.

(40) To no one will we sell, to no one deny or delay right or justice.

**charter of King John**

## It's a Fact!

Clause 54 shows how little power women had. It says a woman's word isn't enough to arrest a person for murder, except in the case of her husband's death.

## HOLDING THE KING ACCOUNTABLE

According to clause 61, if the king or one of his officials breaks any clauses in the Magna Carta, the barons can demand that the king make things right immediately. If the king takes no action within 40 days, the barons can use force against him. They may "**assail** us [the king] in every way possible, with the support of the whole community of the land, by seizing our castles, lands, possessions, or anything else."

Copies of the Magna Carta were read throughout the kingdom. It seemed the barons were victorious. But John wasn't about to let this challenge to his authority stand. In 1216, he went back on the Magna Carta. The furious barons declared war.

The war was short. John died in October 1216, and his 9-year-old son became King Henry III. Henry's advisors made peace with the barons and reissued the Magna Carta. The barons reclaimed their victory.

The Magna Carta is a remarkable document, but you probably noticed that it's about rights and liberty for the barons, not everyone. How did it become something that shaped the American notion of universal rights and liberty? A man born more than 300 years after the Magna Carta is responsible.

King Henry III

## It's a Fact!

Henry III wasn't an effective ruler, and conflicts with the barons continued throughout his reign.

## THE MAGNA CARTA THROUGHOUT THE 13TH CENTURY

Because Henry III was so young when he became king, his advisors feared war with the barons. So they reissued the Magna Carta in 1216 and again in 1217. In 1225, when Henry was old enough to assume his duties as king, he reissued the Magna Carta himself. He issued it again in 1264. In 1297, Edward I increased the Magna Carta's importance by declaring that all judgments contrary to the Great Charter weren't binding.

# EDWARD COKE, CHAMPION of LIBERTY and LAW

Edward Coke (pronounced "Cook") was an English lawyer and judge. He began his career in 1578, but his most important contributions to the history of liberty came between 1606 and his death in 1634.

After serving as a lawyer for the royal court, Coke became a judge in 1606. He was a champion of what's known as common law. This body of law is based on **precedents** established over the centuries by judicial decisions rather than on **statutes** passed by **Parliament** or the king. Coke believed common law was superior to royal authority. He also believed rights and freedoms belonged to everyone, not just to nobles. His decisions as a judge often angered the king, but Coke never backed down.

## It's a Fact!

James I fired Coke from his royal position in 1616. Coke was so desperate to get it back that he forced his 14-year-old daughter to marry a man who could help him.

Edward Coke

# COKE AND THE MONARCHY

When Coke began his career, Elizabeth I was queen of England. Coke was ambitious and wanted power. In 1594, he became the queen's chief lawyer. After her death in 1603, Coke's conflicts with the monarchy began. He opposed King James I's demands for more and more money to pay for his luxurious lifestyle. He also opposed James's attempts to influence court cases. Coke had similar conflicts with Charles I, who became king in 1625.

In his own time, Coke was respected as a brilliant legal thinker but was also known to be a difficult person.

In one of Coke's most famous decisions, he ruled common law was above Parliamentary statutes. He declared judges had the power to pronounce a law **void**.

Coke's Petition of Right, presented to Charles I in 1628, rejected the idea that monarchs are above the law. It declared some of Charles's acts illegal and demanded he honor common law. It claimed liberties for all people based on precedents, including the Magna Carta—which Coke claimed applied to all men, not just barons.

Coke's writings influenced many later generations, including the Founding Fathers of the United States. Men such as Thomas Jefferson, John Adams, Patrick Henry, and James Madison admired Coke's ideas—and they acquired their understanding of the Magna Carta from Coke's writings.

**Petition of Right**

↓

## It's a Fact!

In his ruling on one case, Coke wrote that a man's home is his castle and he has the right to defend it. He even supported rights against searches by the king's sheriffs.

## THE PETITION OF RIGHT

Like the Magna Carta, the petition complained about royal abuses. Coke wrote the king had broken the Great Charter's promise that no man could be arrested, imprisoned, stripped of his land or liberty, or sentenced to death except "by the lawful judgment of his peers, or by the law of the land." He also charged that forced **quartering** of soldiers and failure to apply laws equally to all men were against the laws and customs of England.

19

# The VIRGINIA DECLARATION of RIGHTS

In May 1776, at the request of the Virginia Convention, George Mason wrote a document called the Virginia Declaration of Rights. The document was brief, containing only 16 short sections. Among those sections are several that clearly share the spirit of both the Magna Carta and Coke's writings. Like the earlier documents, Mason's writing proclaims there are limits on the government's power and the people possess rights that can't be taken away.

On June 12, 1776, the Virginia Convention approved the Declaration of Rights, making the spirit of the Magna Carta and Edward Coke part of America. Other colonies copied the Virginia document. Thomas Jefferson drew on it when he wrote the Declaration of Independence. And years later, it formed the basis of the Bill of Rights.

## It's a Fact!

May 1776 was a tense time for England's American colonies. The American Revolution had begun the year before, but the colonies hadn't yet declared their independence.

**George Mason**

George Washington, Thomas Jefferson, and James Madison highly respected Mason, but Mason didn't share the other men's desire for public office.

# PROVISIONS OF THE DECLARATION OF RIGHTS

Can you see how these provisions reflect ideas in the Magna Carta?
- All men are free and have certain basic rights.
- Power comes from the people. Rulers are their servants.
- No man can be deprived of liberty except by the law of the land or the judgment of his peers.
- An accused person is entitled to a speedy trial by a jury of his peers.
- The people have the right to freedom from unreasonable searches and seizures.

21

# The DECLARATION of INDEPENDENCE

When Thomas Jefferson penned the Declaration of Independence in 1776, he drew not only on the Virginia Declaration of Rights, but also on the ideas of Edward Coke and on the Magna Carta. We know how important Coke—and through him, the Magna Carta—was to Jefferson because of Jefferson's letters. Jefferson once wrote that, when he was studying law, all law students read Coke's writings. Jefferson praised Coke's understanding of English liberties in a letter to Madison.

Like the Magna Carta, the Declaration of Independence lists grievances against the king and points out ways he had ignored laws and trampled on the rights of his subjects. And influenced by Coke's ideas, the Declaration of Independence proclaims rights belong to all men, not just a chosen few.

## It's a Fact!

On the eve of the American Revolution, Massachusetts adopted a state seal showing a soldier with a sword in one hand and the Magna Carta in the other.

Benjamin Franklin (left) and John Adams (center) look over Thomas Jefferson's draft of the Declaration of Independence, as Jefferson stands by.

## RIGHTS AND WRONGS

The Declaration of Independence proclaims that all men are created equal, they possess certain basic rights, governments are established to protect these rights, and governments get their power from the consent of the governed. The Declaration also lists abuses of royal power such as the forced quartering of soldiers, taxation without the people's consent, and denying people trial by jury. Look back at the ideas contained in the Magna Carta and Coke's writings. Can you find parallels to these concepts?

# The CONSTITUTION and BILL of RIGHTS

In May 1787, state delegates met in Philadelphia to improve the Articles of **Confederation**, the first constitution of the United States. They soon realized the Articles couldn't be fixed. Instead, they wrote a new constitution.

The Constitution reflects many ideas from the Magna Carta and Edward Coke's writings. Among the justifications for the Constitution listed in the Preamble are to "establish Justice . . . and secure the Blessings of Liberty." The body of the Constitution creates a government whose legislative, executive, and judicial branches have specific powers and also exercise power over each other. This system of checks and balances is designed to limit government power. But it's in the Constitution's Bill of Rights that the Magna Carta's influence is most clearly seen.

## It's a Fact!

The Constitution's Preamble begins with the words "We the People." This was a way of making clear that power is held by the people.

George Washington (right) presided over the Constitutional Convention in Philadelphia, Pennsylvania.

# THE ARTICLES OF CONFEDERATION

The Articles of Confederation was written in 1777 and approved by the states in 1781. But serious flaws quickly became apparent. The central government had so little power it couldn't function effectively. Although the Articles proved to be unworkable, you can see in its desire to limit the central government's power some of the same concerns apparent in the Magna Carta and Edward Coke's writings: fear of a government with so much power that it would deny citizens their rights.

The Bill of Rights is the first 10 amendments to the Constitution. The basic idea—that the people have rights the government can't take away—can be traced back to the Magna Carta. But there are also specific rights that can be found in the Magna Carta and Edward Coke's writings. For example, the Fourth Amendment protects citizens from unreasonable searches and seizures, as did the Magna Carta's clauses 30, 31, and 39. And Coke proclaimed that a man's home is his castle.

The Fifth Amendment promises due process of law. The Magna Carta's clauses 39 and 40 did the same, as did Coke's Petition of Right. The Sixth Amendment promises the right to a speedy trial, a pledge also made by clause 40 of the Magna Carta.

**James Madison**

## It's a Fact!

The Third Amendment protects citizens from being forced to quarter soldiers. Coke demanded this right in his Petition of Right.

# CREATING THE BILL OF RIGHTS

Some delegates complained loudly that the Constitution lacked any declaration of rights. They felt the way was open for the government to abuse its power without such a declaration. George Mason, the author of the Virginia Declaration of Rights, felt such a declaration was absolutely necessary. Some states refused to approve the Constitution until they were assured that a list of rights would be added. James Madison wrote the amendments, and, after approval by the states, the Bill of Rights was added in 1791.

James Madison is called the Father of the Constitution for his work on the document. He also penned the Bill of Rights.

# ENDURING PRINCIPLES of LIBERTY

In 1215, when the English nobles crafted the Articles of the Barons and forced King John to sign them, they weren't trying to establish new rights or new principles of law. They were trying to reclaim rights that had belonged to barons for generations. The clauses in the Magna Carta revered today weren't even the ones most important to the barons.

The clauses we honor are mostly brief, and they appear in the second half of the document. But these clauses of basic rights and liberties became increasingly significant as people looked for precedents to support them in their struggles against tyranny. They ensured the Magna Carta became a document remembered for establishing cherished principles of liberty.

← **Magna Carta**

## It's a Fact!

Today, we expect legal officials to be people who know the law. But it wasn't always that way. In the Magna Carta, King John had to promise to appoint only men who knew the law and meant to observe it.

# TIMELINE OF THE MAGNA CARTA, AN INFLUENTIAL DOCUMENT

**1199**
John becomes king of England

**1297**
Edward I gives the Magna Carta increased power

**1787**
US Constitution is written to reflect Magna Carta ideas

**1776**
George Mason's Virginia Declaration of Rights includes Magna Carta concepts

**1216**
Henry III's advisors reissue the Magna Carta

**1215**
Barons force King John to sign the Magna Carta

**1628**
Edward Coke claims the rights of the Magna Carta apply to all men in his Petition of Right

**1791**
Bill of Rights added to the Constitution; guarantees many rights included in the Magna Carta

**1776**
Thomas Jefferson draws on the Magna Carta for the Declaration of Independence

**1225**
Henry III reissues the Magna Carta

## WHERE CAN YOU SEE THE MAGNA CARTA?

Today, four copies of the 1215 Magna Carta still exist. All four are in England. Two are in the British Museum, one is in Lincoln Cathedral, and one is in Salisbury Cathedral. Durham Cathedral in England has copies of the 1216, 1217, and 1225 documents. But you don't have to go all the way to England to see the Great Charter. The National **Archives** in Washington, DC, has a copy of the 1297 Magna Carta.

# GLOSSARY

**abuse:** a misuse of power that is often illegal

**archives:** a place where records are stored

**assail:** to attack

**charter:** a written statement describing the rights and responsibilities of a government and its citizens

**confederation:** a league of people or states that support each other and act together

**credible:** reliable, believable

**deprive:** to take something away from

**document:** a formal piece of writing

**medieval:** having to do with the period of the Middle Ages in Europe, which lasted from about 500 to 1500

**Parliament:** the law-making body of England

**precedent:** something done or said in the past that sets a model for the future

**quarter:** to provide with lodging or shelter

**statute:** a law

**void:** having no legal force

# FOR MORE INFORMATION

## BOOKS

Baxter, Roberta. *The Magna Carta: Cornerstone of the Constitution.* Chicago, IL: Heinemann Library, 2012.

Danziger, Danny, and John Gillingham. *1215: The Year of Magna Carta.* New York, NY: Simon & Schuster, 2004.

Vincent, Nicholas. *Magna Carta: A Very Short Introduction.* Oxford, England: Oxford University Press, 2012.

## WEBSITES

**Magna Carta—1215**
*www.middle-ages.org.uk/magna-carta.htm*
Read about the Magna Carta, the events leading up to it, and the people involved.

**The Meaning of Magna Carta Since 1215**
*www.historytoday.com/ralph-v-turner/meaning-magna-carta-1215*
Read about the effect of the Magna Carta over the centuries.

**Treasures in Full: Magna Carta**
*www.bl.uk/treasures/magnacarta/index.html*
Examine a copy of the Magna Carta in the British Library, and read a complete English translation of the Latin original.

# INDEX